GOSPEL
Hymns for Ukulele

ISBN 978-1-4584-2341-2

HAL•LEONARD®

7777 W. BLUEMOUND RD. P.O. BOX 13819 MILWAUKEE, WI 53213

In Australia Contact:
Hal Leonard Australia Pty. Ltd.
4 Lentara Court
Cheltenham, Victoria, 3192 Australia
Email: ausadmin@halleonard.com.au

Visit Hal Leonard Online at
www.halleonard.com

Amazing Grace

Words by John Newton
Traditional American Melody

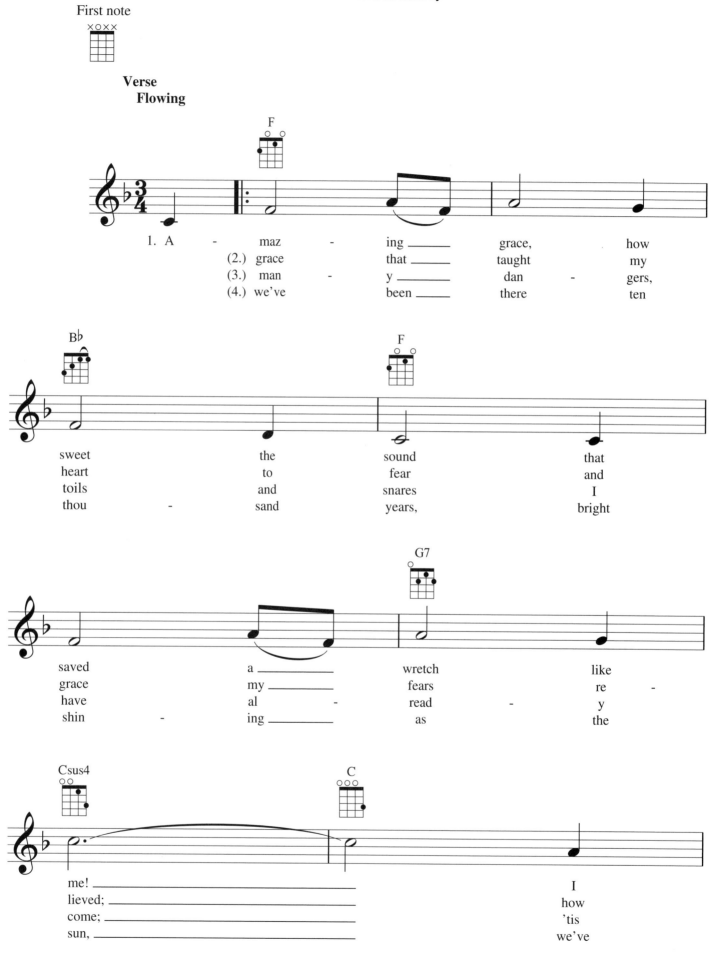

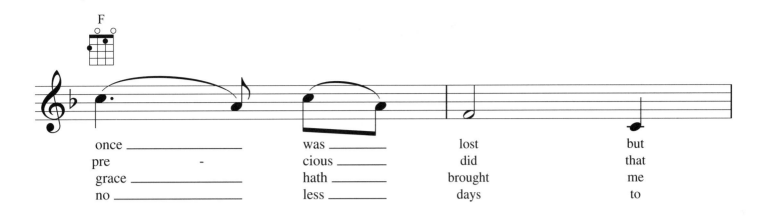

once _____ was _____ lost but
pre - cious _____ did that
grace _____ hath _____ brought me
no _____ less _____ days to

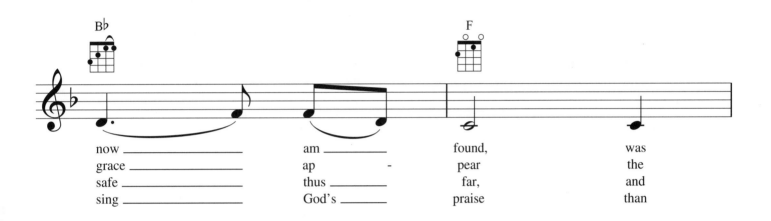

now _____ am _____ found, was
grace _____ ap - pear the
safe _____ thus _____ far, and
sing _____ God's _____ praise than

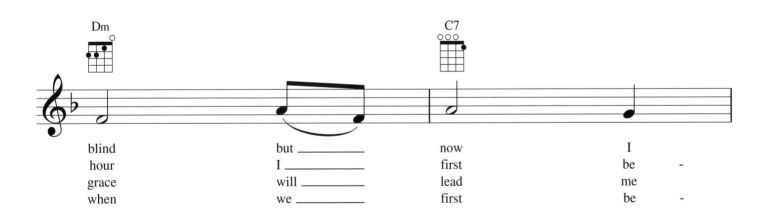

blind but _____ now I
hour I _____ first be -
grace will _____ lead me
when we _____ first be -

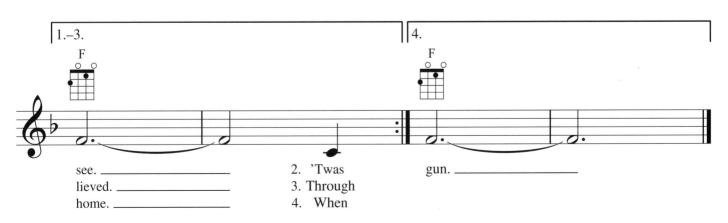

see. _____ 2. 'Twas gun. _____
lieved. _____ 3. Through
home. _____ 4. When

3

At Calvary

Words by William R. Newell
Music by Daniel B. Towner

First note

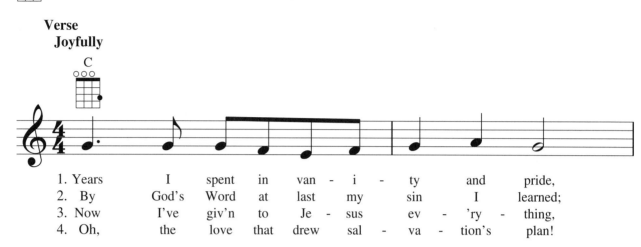

Verse
Joyfully

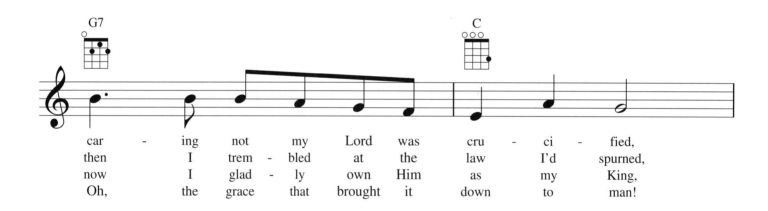

1. Years   I   spent   in   van - i - ty   and   pride,
2. By   God's   Word   at   last   my   sin   I   learned;
3. Now   I've   giv'n   to   Je - sus   ev - 'ry - thing,
4. Oh,   the   love   that   drew   sal - va - tion's   plan!

car - ing   not   my   Lord   was   cru - ci - fied,
then   I   trem - bled   at   the   law   I'd   spurned,
now   I   glad - ly   own   Him   as   my   King,
Oh,   the   grace   that   brought   it   down   to   man!

know - ing   not   it   was   for   me   He   died   on
till   my   guilt - y   soul   im - plor - ing   turned   to
now   my   rap - tured   soul   can   on - ly   sing   of
Oh,   the   might - y   gulf   that   God   did   span   at

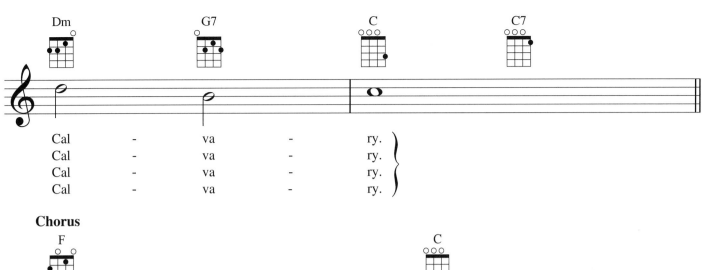

Cal - va - ry.
Cal - va - ry.
Cal - va - ry.
Cal - va - ry.

Chorus

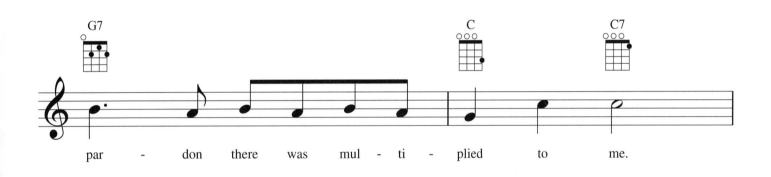

Mer - cy there was great and grace was free,

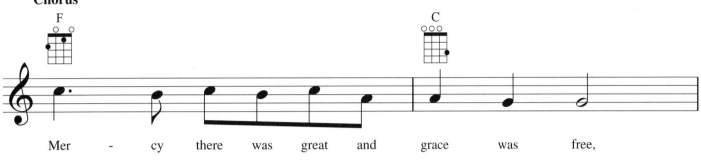

par - don there was mul - ti - plied to me.

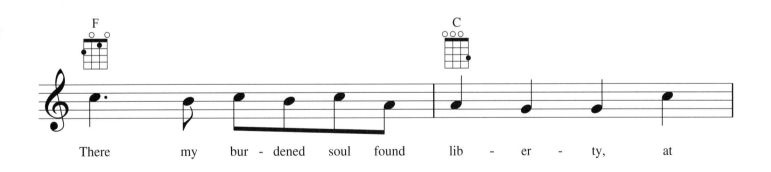

There my bur - dened soul found lib - er - ty, at

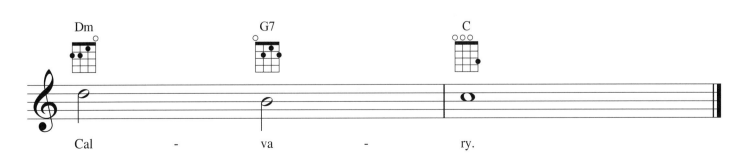

Cal - va - ry.

Blessed Assurance

Lyrics by Fanny J. Crosby
Music by Phoebe Palmer Knapp

First note

Verse
Joyfully

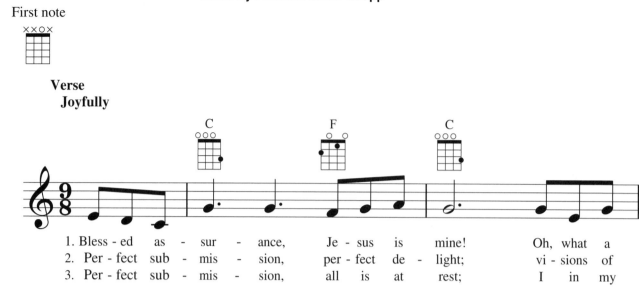

1. Bless - ed as - sur - ance, Je - sus is mine! Oh, what a
2. Per - fect sub - mis - sion, per - fect de - light; vi - sions of
3. Per - fect sub - mis - sion, all is at rest; I in my

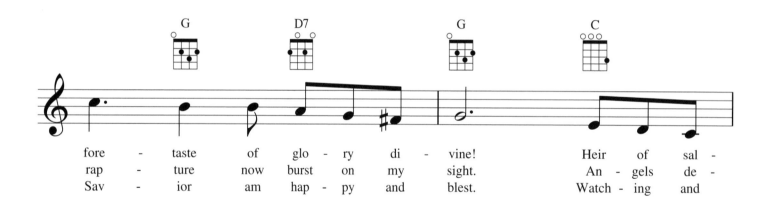

fore - taste of glo - ry di - vine! Heir of sal -
rap - ture now burst on my sight. An - gels de -
Sav - ior am hap - py and blest. Watch - ing and

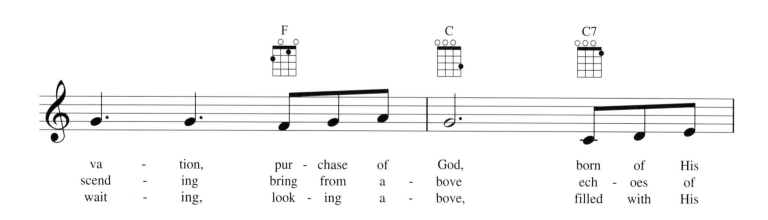

va - tion, pur - chase of God, born of His
scend - ing bring from a - bove ech - oes of
wait - ing, look - ing a - bove, filled with His

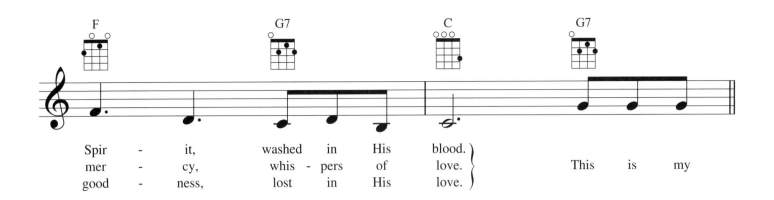

Chorus

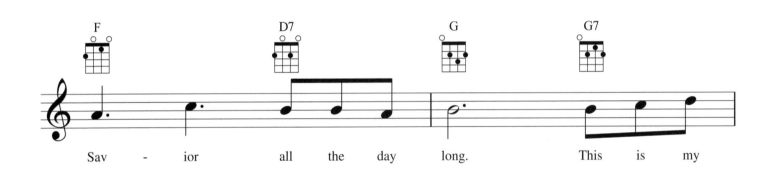

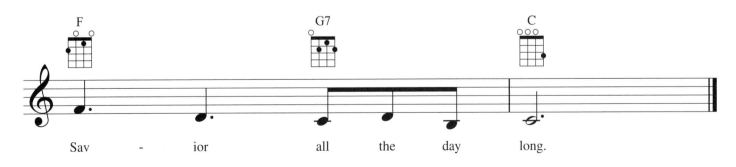

Down at the Cross
(Glory to His Name)

Words by Elisha A. Hoffman
Music by John H. Stockton

First note

Verse
Brightly

1. Down at the cross where my Sav - ior died,
2. I am so won - drous - ly saved from sin,
3. O pre - cious foun - tain that saves from sin,
4. Come to this foun - tain so rich and sweet,

down where for cleans - ing from sin I cried,
Je - sus so sweet - ly a - bides with - in,
I am so glad that I en - tered in.
cast thy poor soul at the Sav - ior's feet.

there to my heart was the blood ap - plied;
there at the cross where He took me in;
There Je - sus saves me and keeps me clean;
Plunge in to - day and be made com - plete;

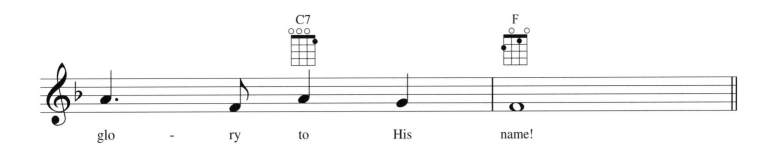

glo - ry to His name!

Chorus

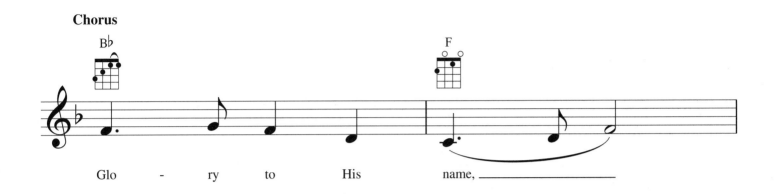

Glo - ry to His name, _____

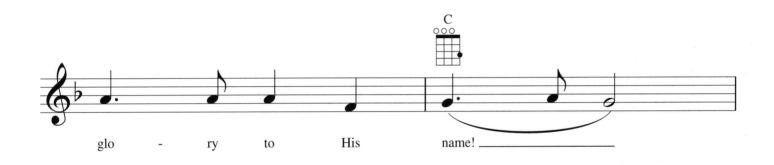

glo - ry to His name! _____

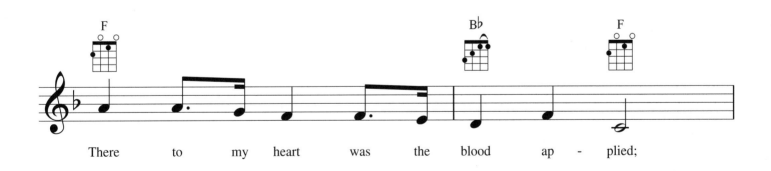

There to my heart was the blood ap - plied;

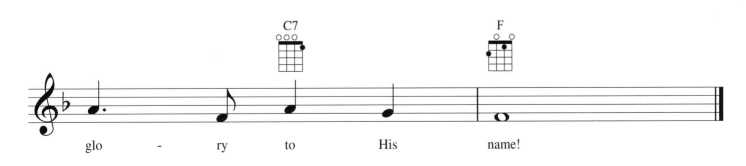

glo - ry to His name!

Footsteps of Jesus

Words by Mary B.C. Slade
Music by Asa B. Everett

First note

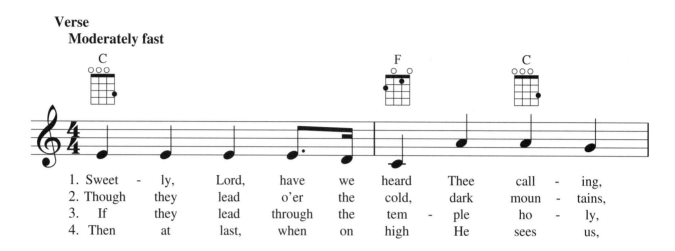

Verse
Moderately fast

1. Sweet - ly, Lord, have we heard Thee call - ing,
2. Though they lead o'er the cold, dark moun - tains,
3. If they lead through the tem - ple ho - ly,
4. Then at last, when on high He sees us,

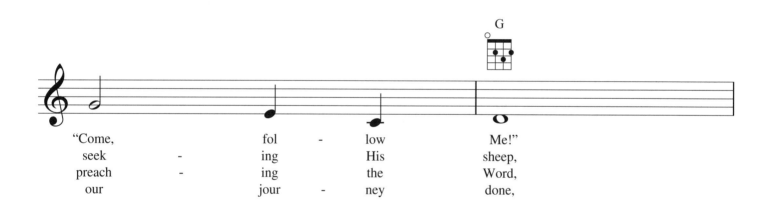

"Come, fol - low Me!"
seek - ing His sheep,
preach - ing the Word,
our jour - ney done,

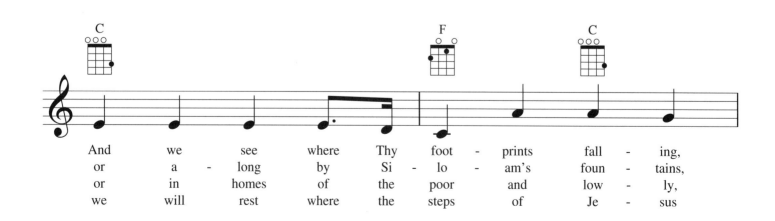

And we see where Thy foot - prints fall - ing,
or a - long by Si - lo - am's foun - tains,
or in homes of the poor and low - ly,
we will rest where the steps of Je - sus

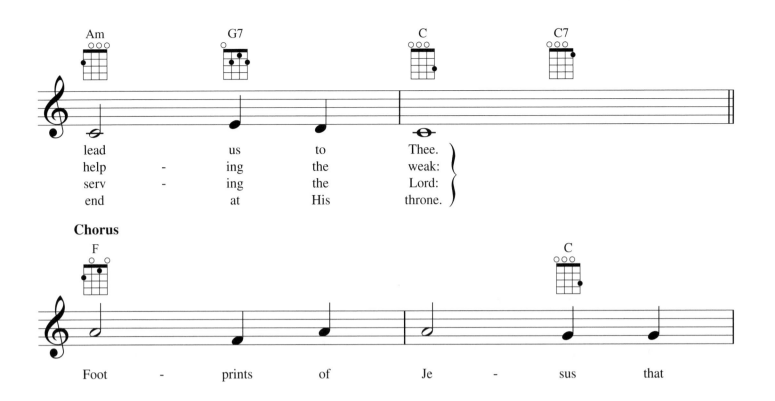

Chorus

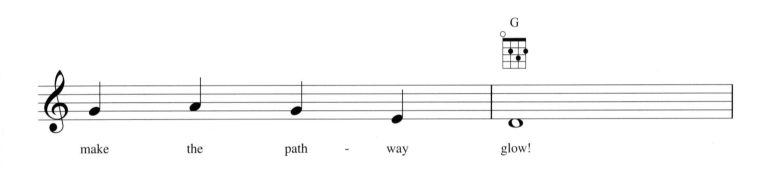

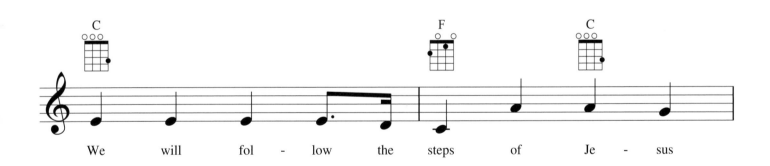

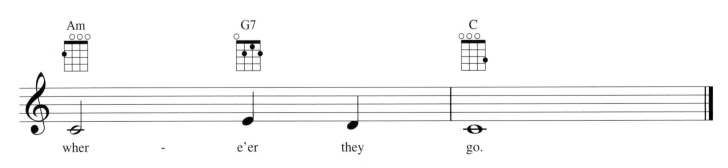

He Keeps Me Singing

Words and Music by Luther B. Bridgers

First note

1. There's with - in my heart a mel - o - dy;
2. All my life was wrecked by sin and strife;
3. Feast - ing on the rich - es of His grace,
4. Though some - times He leads through wa - ters deep,
5. Soon He's com - ing back to wel - come me,

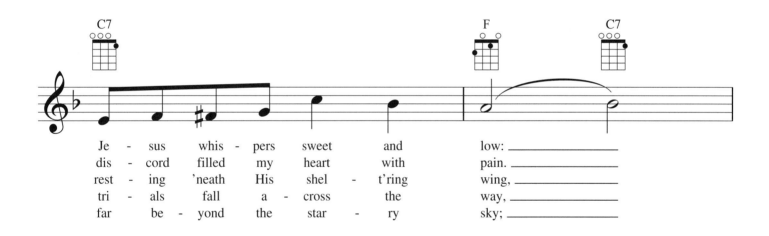

Je - sus whis - pers sweet and low: _____
dis - cord filled my heart with pain. _____
rest - ing 'neath His shel - t'ring wing, _____
tri - als fall a - cross the way, _____
far be - yond the star - ry sky; _____

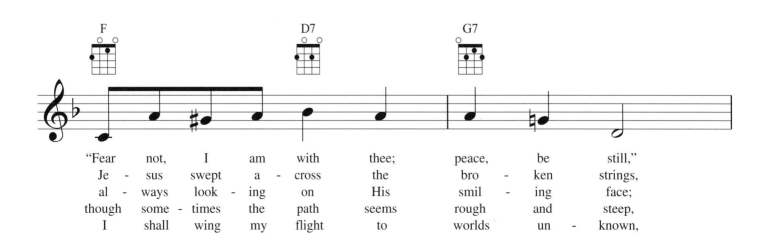

"Fear not, I am with thee; peace, be still,"
Je - sus swept a - cross the bro - ken strings,
al - ways look - ing on His smil - ing face;
though some - times the path seems rough and steep,
I shall wing my flight to worlds un - known,

in all of life's ebb and flow.
stirred all the slum - b'ring chords a - gain.
that is why I shout and sing.
see His foot - prints all the way.
I shall reign with Him on high.

Chorus

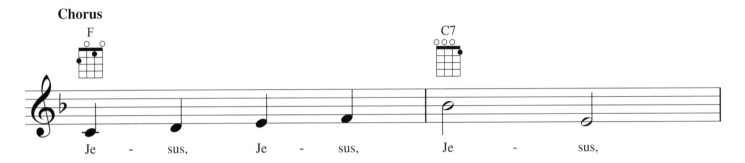

Je - sus, Je - sus, Je - sus,

sweet - est name I know;

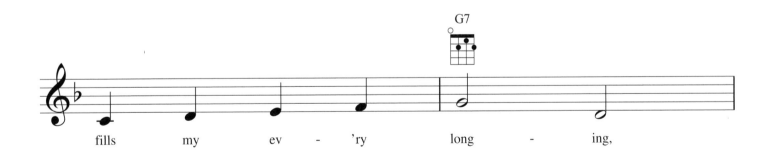

fills my ev - 'ry long - ing,

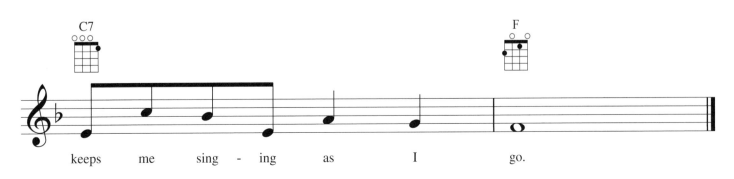

keeps me sing - ing as I go.

Heavenly Sunlight

Words by Henry J. Zelley
Music by George Harrison Cook

First note

Verse
Brightly

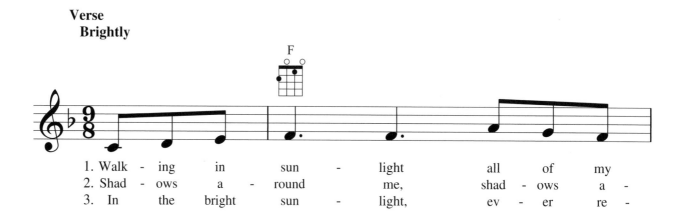

1. Walk - ing in sun - light all of my
2. Shad - ows a - round me, shad - ows a -
3. In the bright sun - light, ev - er re -

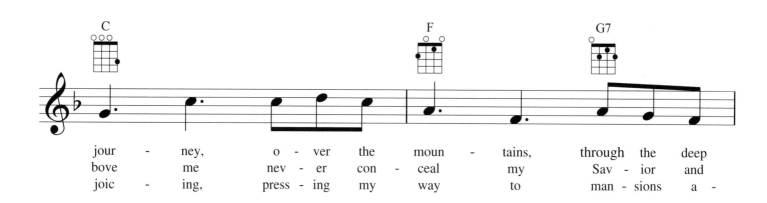

jour - ney, o - ver the moun - tains, through the deep
bove me nev - er con - ceal my Sav - ior and
joic - ing, press - ing my way to man - sions a -

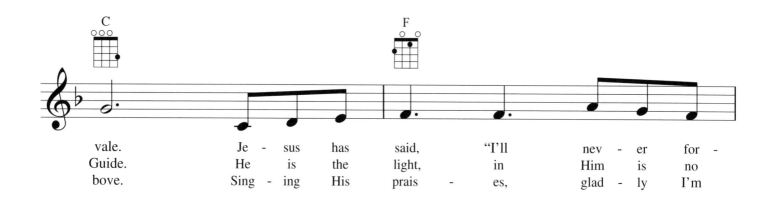

vale. Je - sus has said, "I'll nev - er for -
Guide. He is the light, in Him is no
bove. Sing - ing His prais - es, glad - ly I'm

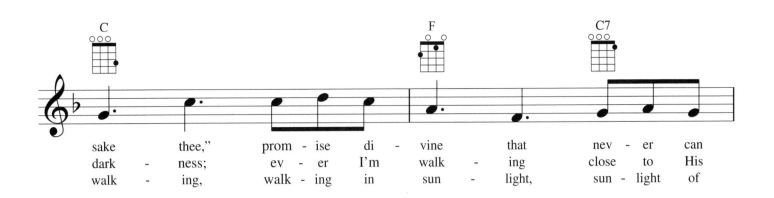

sake thee," prom - ise di - vine that nev - er can
dark - ness; ev - er I'm walk - ing close to His
walk - ing, walk - ing in sun - light, sun - light of

Chorus

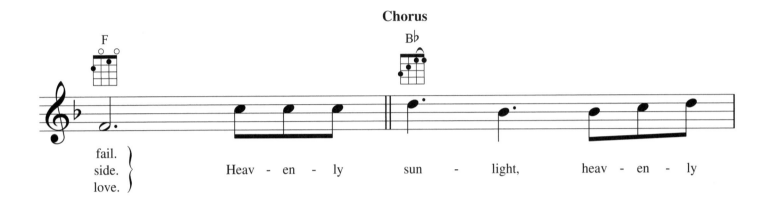

fail.
side.
love.

Heav - en - ly sun - light, heav - en - ly

sun - light, flood - ing my soul with glo - ry di -

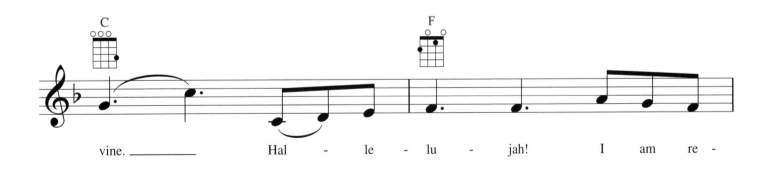

vine. _____ Hal - le - lu - jah! I am re -

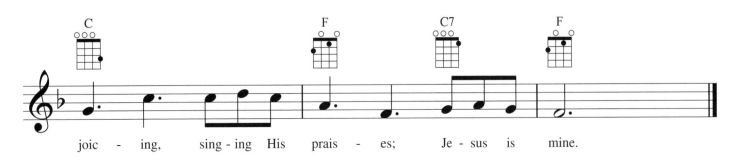

joic - ing, sing - ing His prais - es; Je - sus is mine.

His Eye Is on the Sparrow

Words by Civilla D. Martin
Music by Charles H. Gabriel

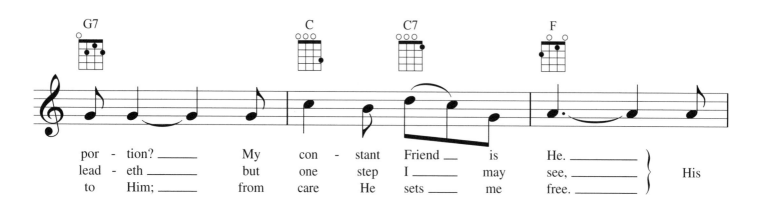

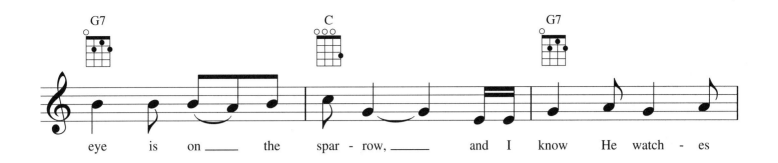

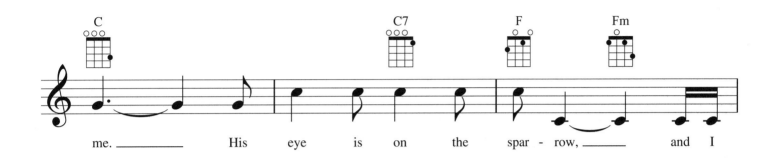

Chorus

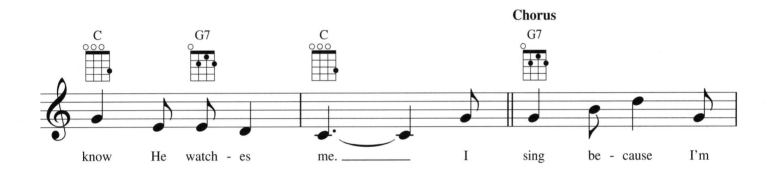

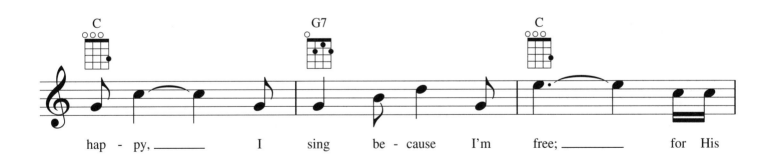

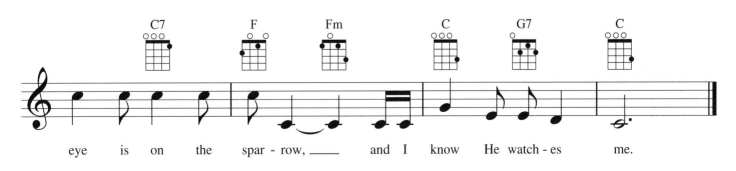

In the Garden

Words and Music by C. Austin Miles

Chorus

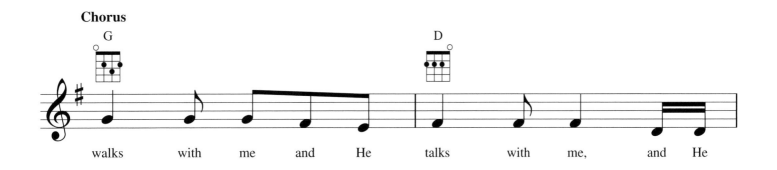

walks with me and He talks with me, and He

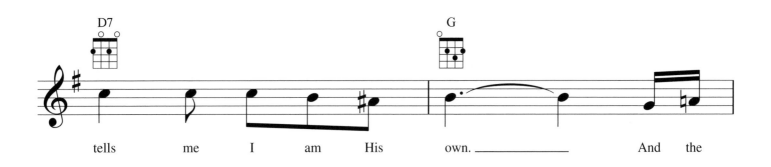

tells me I am His own. _____ And the

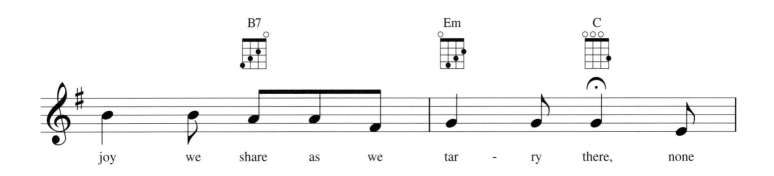

joy we share as we tar - ry there, none

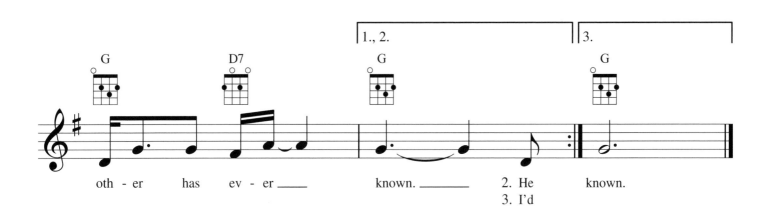

oth - er has ev - er _____ known. _____ 2. He known.
3. I'd

Jesus Paid It All

Words by Elvina M. Hall
Music by John T. Grape

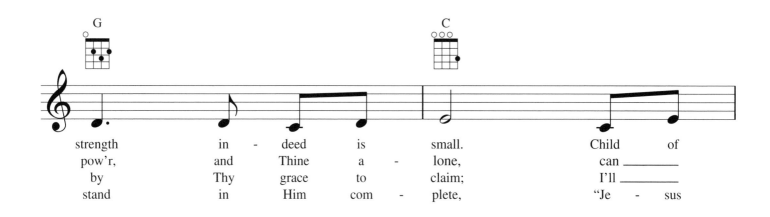

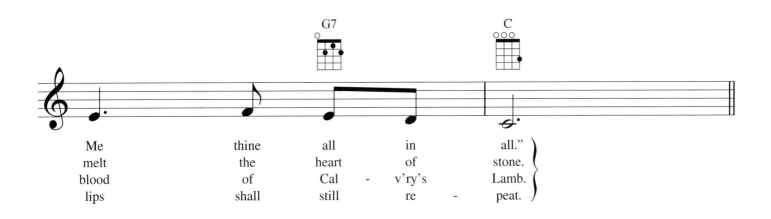

Me thine all in all."
melt the heart of stone.
blood of Cal - v'ry's Lamb.
lips shall still re - peat.

Chorus

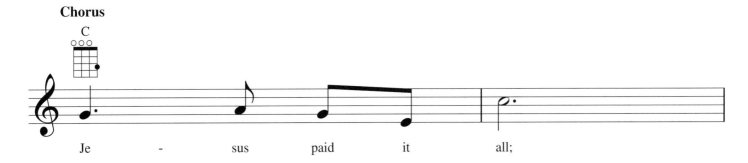

Je - sus paid it all;

all to Him I owe.

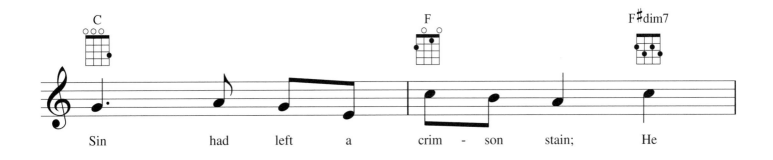

Sin had left a crim - son stain; He

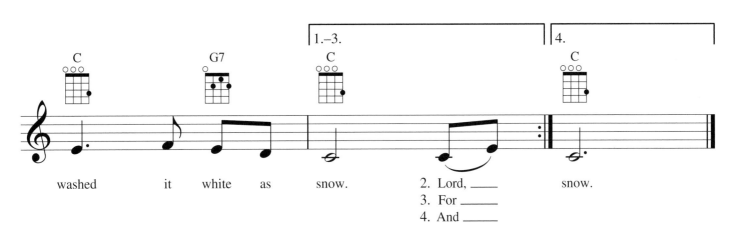

washed it white as snow. 2. Lord, _____ snow.
3. For _____
4. And _____

Just a Closer Walk with Thee

Traditional
Arranged by Kenneth Morris

First note

1. I am weak, but Thou art strong.
2. Through this world of toil and snares,
3. When my fee - ble life is o'er,

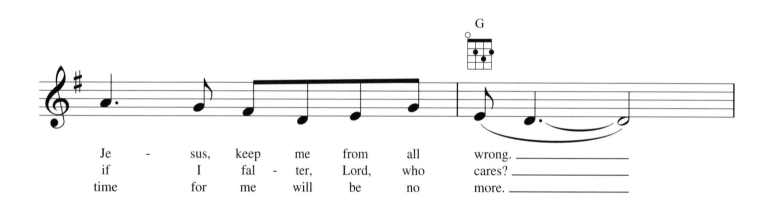

Je - sus, keep me from all wrong. _____
if I fal - ter, Lord, who cares? _____
time for me will be no more. _____

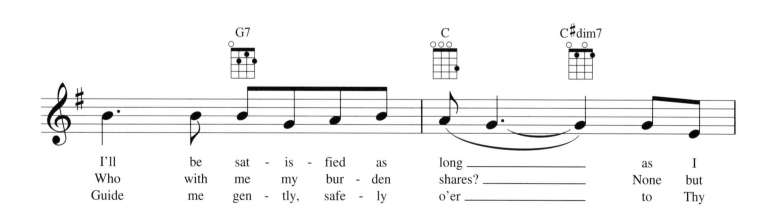

I'll be sat - is - fied as long _____ as I
Who with me my bur - den shares? _____ None but
Guide me gen - tly, safe - ly o'er _____ to Thy

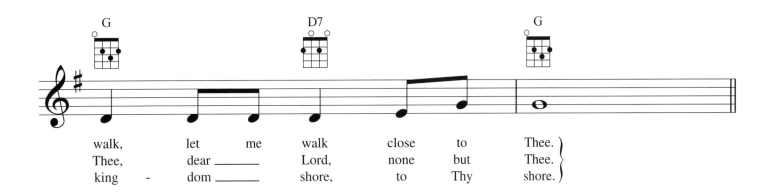

Chorus

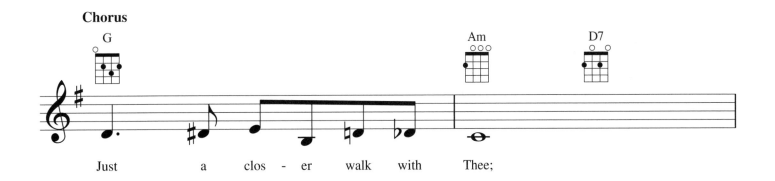

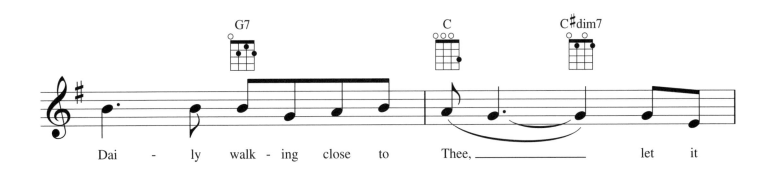

Leaning on the Everlasting Arms

Words by Elisha A. Hoffman
Music by Anthony J. Showalter

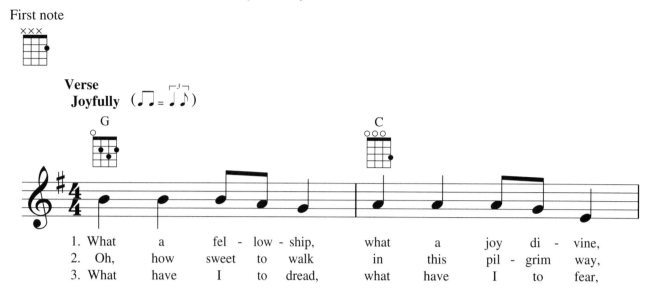

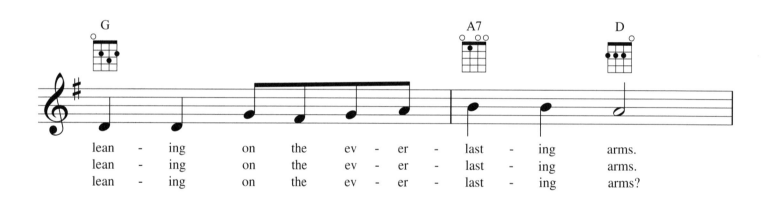

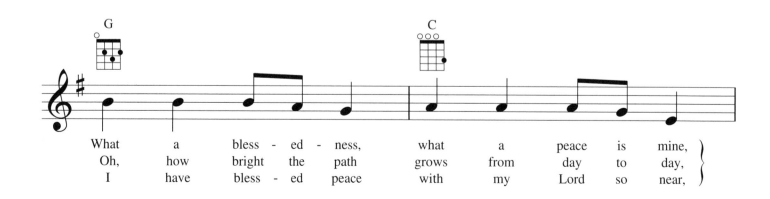

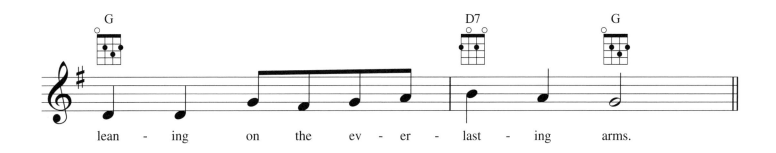

lean - ing on the ev - er - last - ing arms.

Chorus

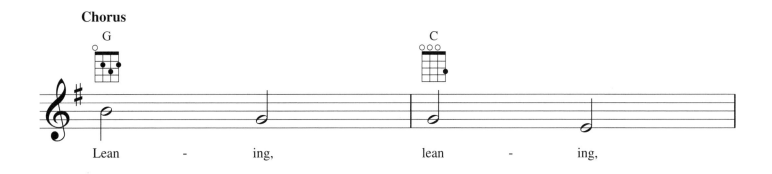

Lean - ing, lean - ing,

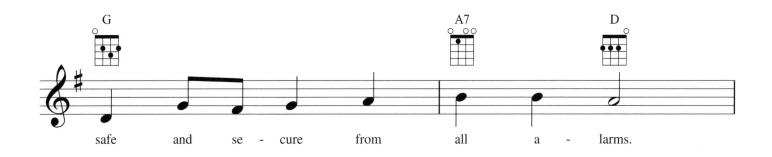

safe and se - cure from all a - larms.

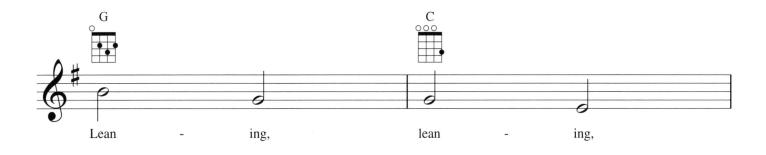

Lean - ing, lean - ing,

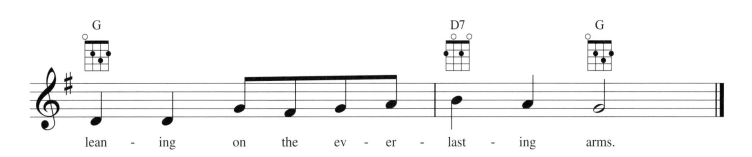

lean - ing on the ev - er - last - ing arms.

The Love of God

Words by Frederick M. Lehman and Meir Ben Isaac Nehorai
Music by Frederick M. Lehman

First note

Verse
Warmly

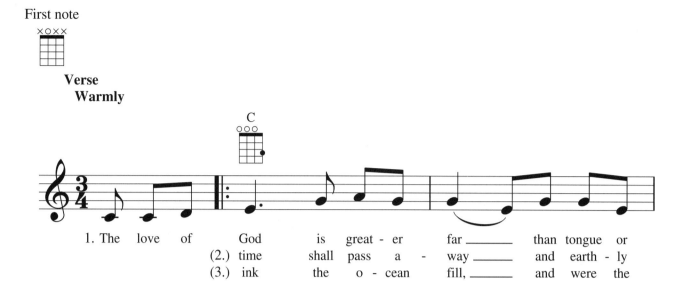

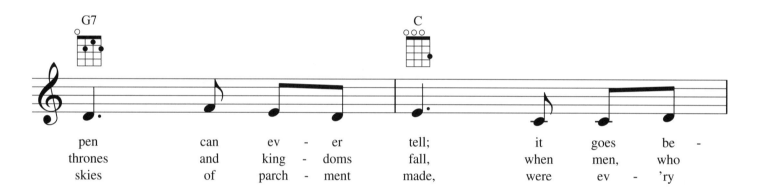

1. The love of God   is great-er far _____ than tongue or
(2.) time shall pass a - way _____ and earth - ly
(3.) ink the o - cean fill, _____ and were the

pen   can   ev - er   tell;   it   goes   be -
thrones   and   king - doms   fall,   when   men,   who
skies   of   parch - ment   made,   were   ev - 'ry

yond   the   high - est   star _____ and   reach - es   to   the   low - est
here   re - fuse   to   pray, _____ on   rocks   and   hills   and   moun - tains
stalk   on   earth   a   quill _____ and   ev - 'ry   man   a   scribe   by

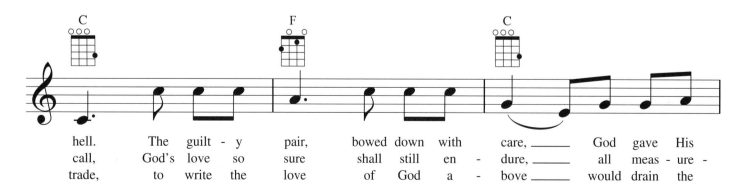

hell.   The   guilt - y   pair,   bowed   down   with   care, _____ God   gave   His
call,   God's   love   so   sure   shall   still   en - dure, _____ all   meas - ure -
trade,   to   write   the   love   of   God   a - bove _____ would   drain   the

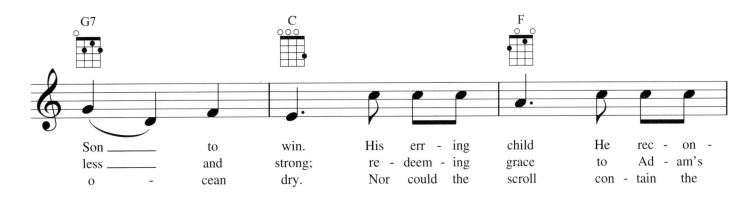

Son _____ to win. His err - ing child He rec - on -
less _____ and strong; re - deem - ing grace to Ad - am's
o - cean dry. Nor could the scroll con - tain the

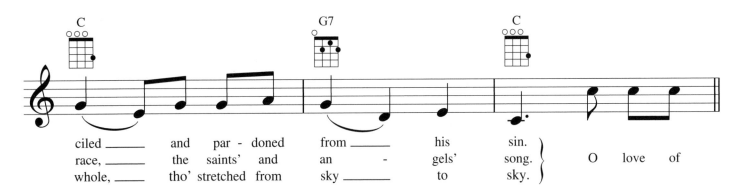

ciled _____ and par - doned from _____ his sin. }
race, _____ the saints' and an - gels' song. } O love of
whole, _____ tho' stretched from sky _____ to sky. }

Chorus

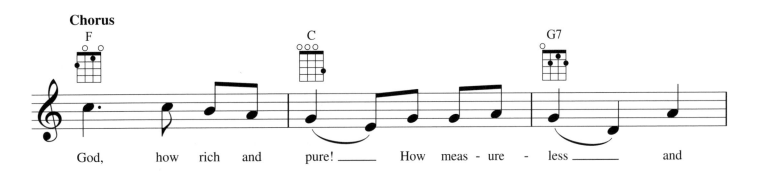

God, how rich and pure! _____ How meas - ure - less _____ and

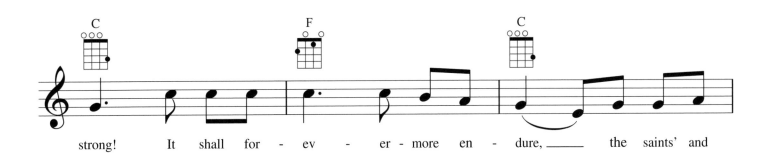

strong! It shall for - ev - er - more en - dure, _____ the saints' and

1., 2.   3.

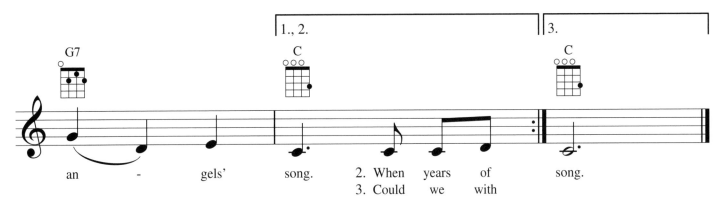

an - gels' song. 2. When years of song.
3. Could we with

My Hope Is Built on Nothing Less

Words by Edward Mote
Music by William B. Bradbury

First note

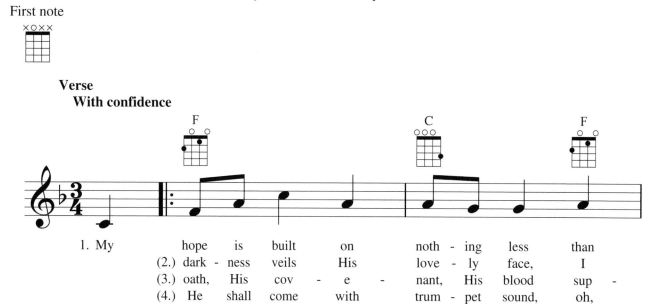

Verse
With confidence

1. My hope is built on noth - ing less than
(2.) dark - ness veils His love - ly face, I
(3.) oath, His cov - e - nant, His blood sup -
(4.) He shall come with trum - pet sound, oh,

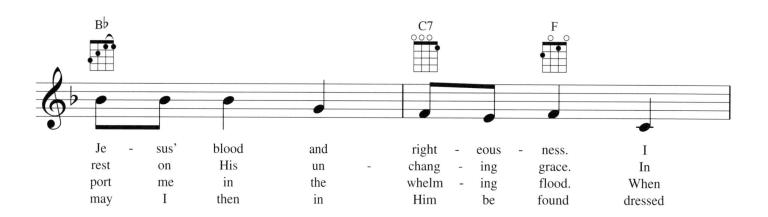

Je - sus' blood and right - eous - ness. I
rest on His un - chang - ing grace. In
port me in the whelm - ing flood. When
may I then in Him be found dressed

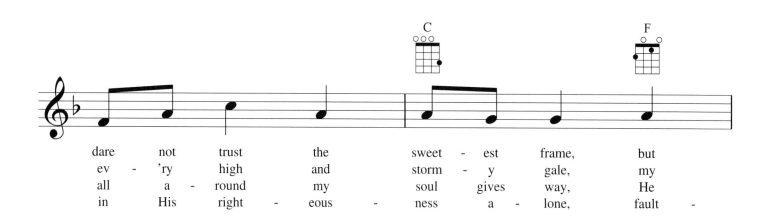

dare not trust the sweet - est frame, but
ev - 'ry high and storm - y gale, my
all a - round my soul gives way, He
in His right - eous - ness a - lone, fault -

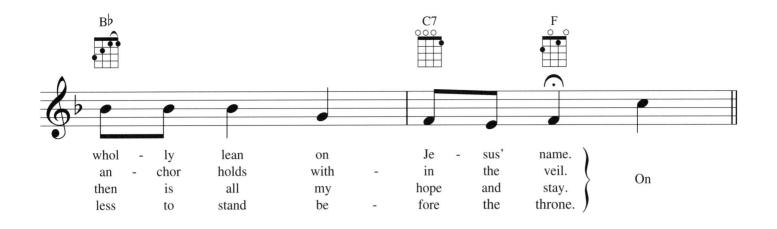

whol - ly lean on Je - sus' name.
an - chor holds with - in the veil.
then is all my hope and stay.
less to stand be - fore the throne.

} On

Chorus

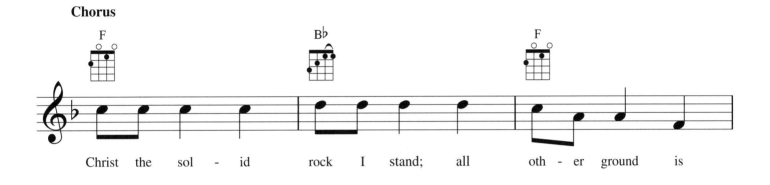

Christ the sol - id rock I stand; all oth - er ground is

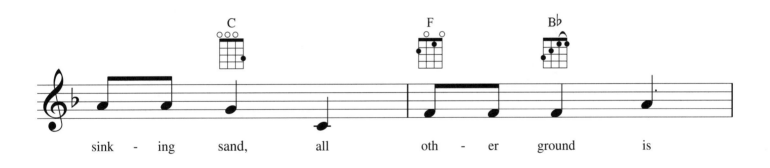

sink - ing sand, all oth - er ground is

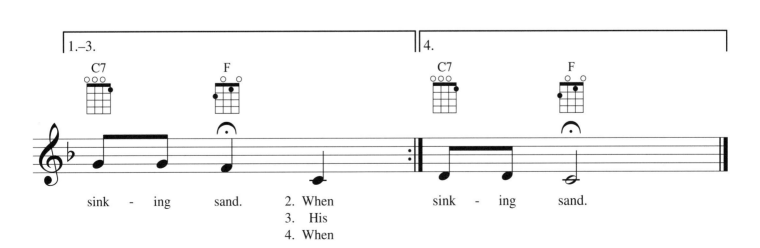

1.–3.

sink - ing sand. 2. When
3. His
4. When

4.

sink - ing sand.

Near the Cross

Words by Fanny J. Crosby
Music by William H. Doane

First note

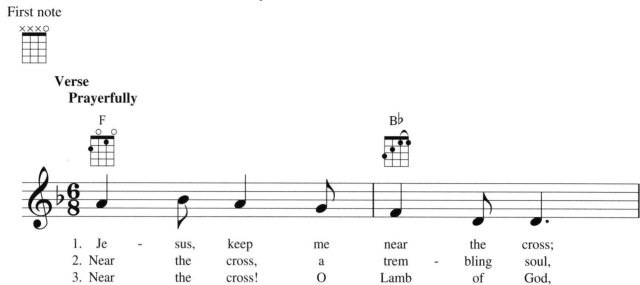

Verse
Prayerfully

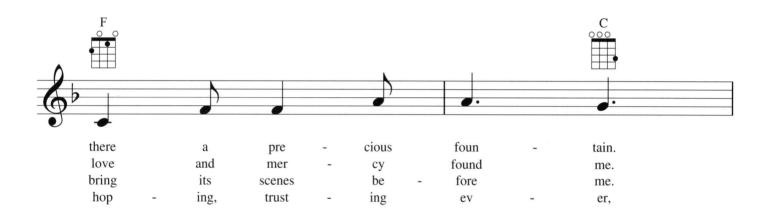

1. Je - sus,	keep	me	near	the	cross;
2. Near	the	cross,	a	trem - bling	soul,
3. Near	the	cross!	O	Lamb	of	God,
4. Near	the	cross	I'll	watch	and	wait,

there a pre - cious foun - tain.
love and mer - cy found me.
bring its scenes be - fore me.
hop - ing, trust - ing ev - er,

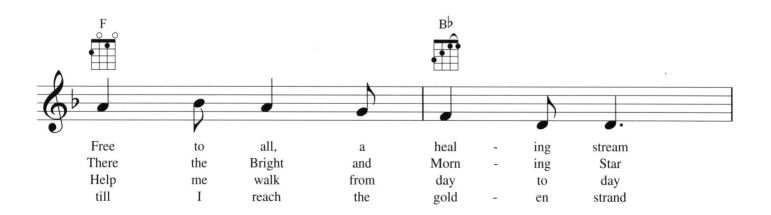

Free to all, a heal - ing stream
There to the Bright and Morn - ing Star
Help me walk from day to day
till I reach the gold - en strand

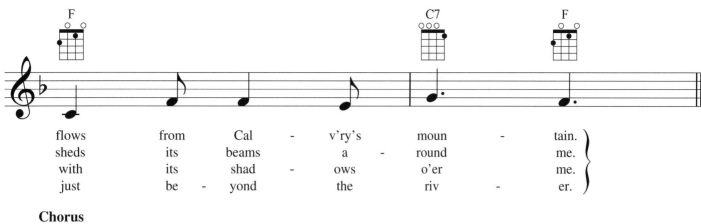

flows from Cal - v'ry's moun - tain.
sheds its beams a - round me.
with its shad - ows o'er me.
just be - yond the riv - er.

Chorus

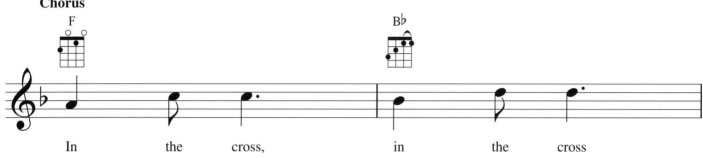

In the cross, in the cross

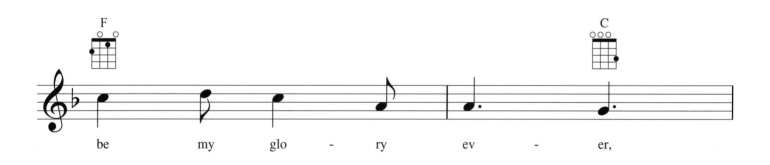

be my glo - ry ev - er,

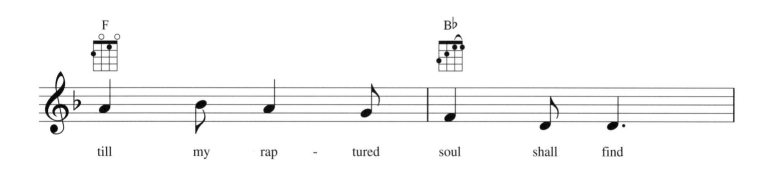

till my rap - tured soul shall find

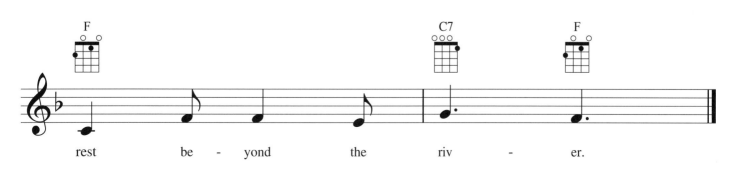

rest be - yond the riv - er.

Nothing But the Blood

Words and Music by Robert Lowry

First note

Verse
Moderately fast

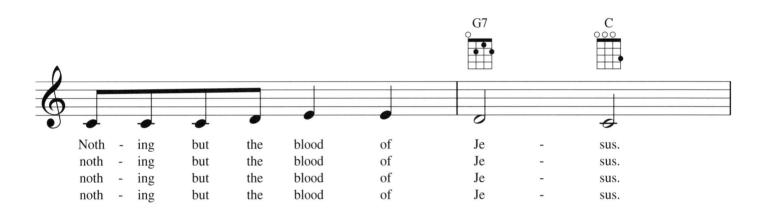

1. What can wash a - way my sin?
2. For my par - don this I see:
3. Noth - ing can for sin a - tone,
4. This is all my hope and peace:

Noth - ing but the blood of Je - sus.
noth - ing but the blood of Je - sus.
noth - ing but the blood of Je - sus.
noth - ing but the blood of Je - sus.

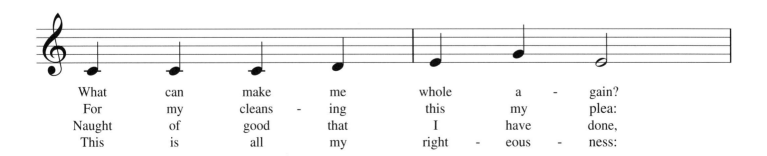

What can make me whole a - gain?
For my cleans - ing this my plea:
Naught of good that I have done,
This is all my right - eous - ness:

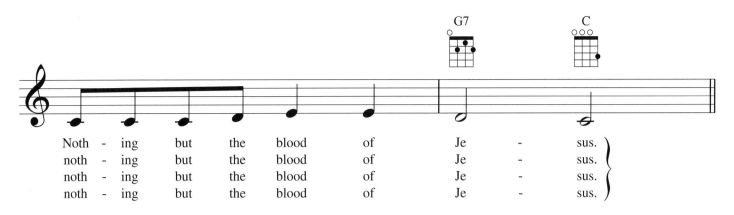

Noth - ing but the blood of Je - sus.
noth - ing but the blood of Je - sus.
noth - ing but the blood of Je - sus.
noth - ing but the blood of Je - sus.

Chorus

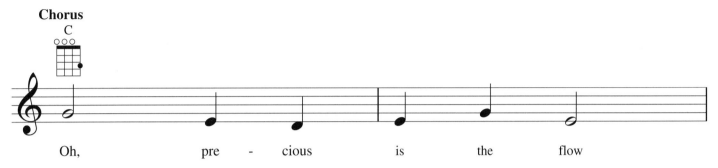

Oh, pre - cious is the flow

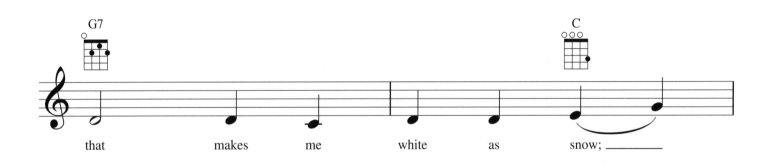

that makes me white as snow; _____

no oth - er fount I know,

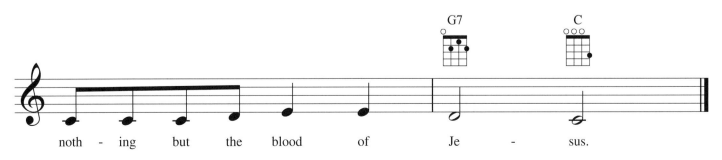

noth - ing but the blood of Je - sus.

The Old Rugged Cross

Words and Music by Rev. George Bennard

First note

Verse
Reflectively

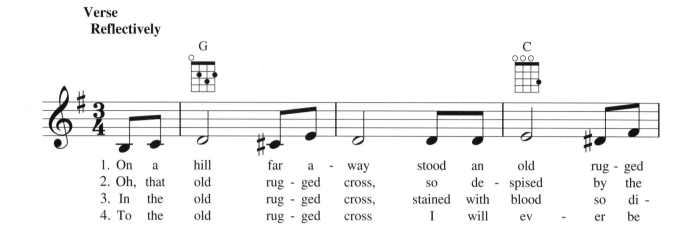

1. On a hill far a - way stood an old rug - ged
2. Oh, that old rug - ged cross, so de - spised by the
3. In the old rug - ged cross, stained with blood so di -
4. To the old rug - ged cross I will ev - er be

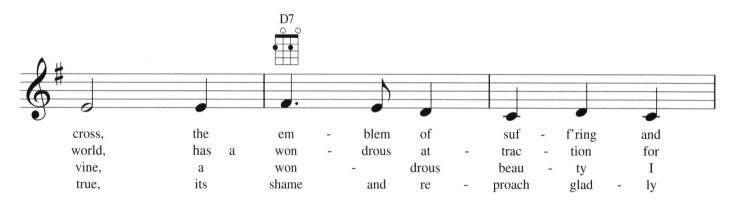

cross, the em - blem of suf - f'ring and
world, has a won - drous at - trac - tion for
vine, a won - drous beau - ty I
true, its shame and re - proach glad - ly

shame. _____ And I love that old
me, _____ for the dear Lamb of
see, _____ for 'twas on that old
bear. _____ Then He'll call me some -

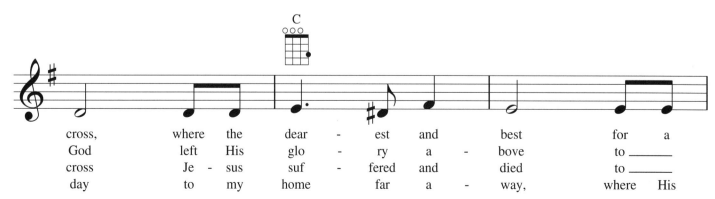

cross, where the dear - est and best for a
God left His glo - ry a - bove to _____
cross Je - sus suf - fered and died to _____
day to my home far a - way, where His

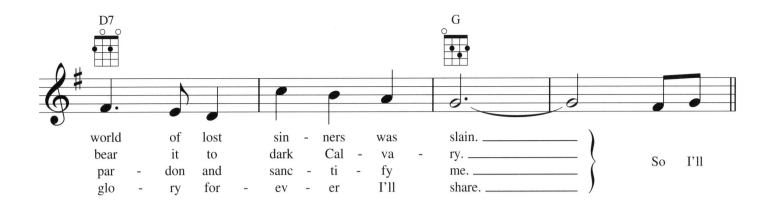

world   of   lost   sin - ners   was   slain. _____
bear   it   to   dark   Cal - va -   ry. _____
par - don and   sanc - ti - fy   me. _____
glo - ry for - ev - er   I'll   share. _____

So I'll

Chorus

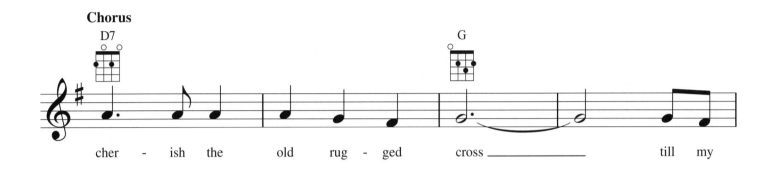

cher - ish the   old   rug - ged   cross _____   till my

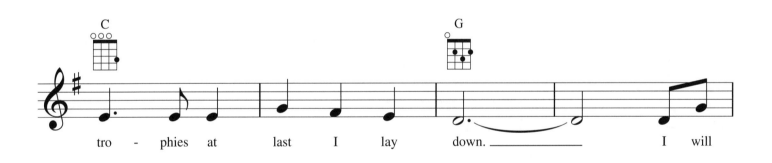

tro - phies at   last   I   lay   down. _____   I will

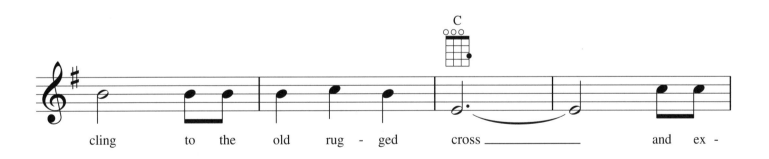

cling   to   the   old   rug - ged   cross _____   and ex -

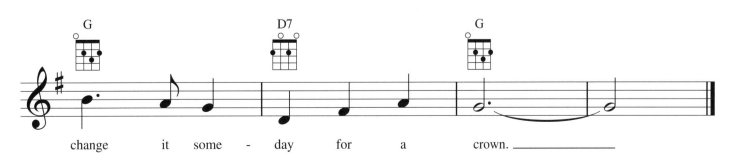

change   it   some - day for   a   crown. _____

35

Shall We Gather at the River?

Words and Music by Robert Lowry

First note

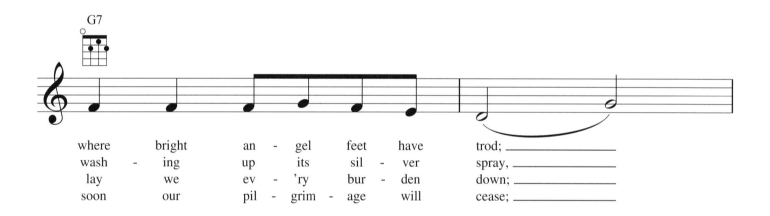

1. Shall we gath - er at the riv - er,
2. On the mar - gin of the riv - er,
3. Ere we reach the shin - ing riv - er,
4. Soon we'll reach the shin - ing riv - er,

where bright an - gel feet have trod; _____
wash - ing up its sil - ver spray, _____
lay we ev - 'ry bur - den down; _____
soon our pil - grim - age will cease; _____

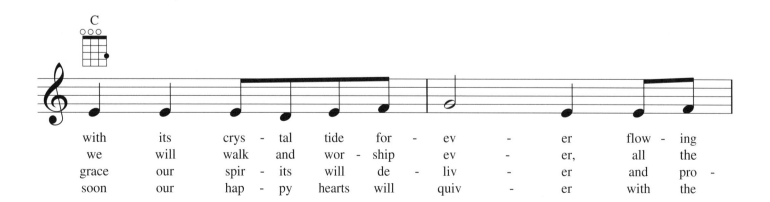

with its crys - tal tide for - ev - er flow - ing
we will walk and wor - ship ev - er, all the
grace our spir - its will de - liv - er and pro -
soon our hap - py hearts will quiv - er with the

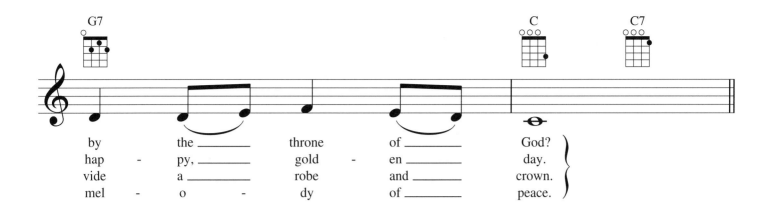

by   the _____   throne   of _____   God?
hap - py, _____   gold - en _____   day.
vide   a _____   robe   and _____   crown.
mel - o - dy   of _____   peace.

Chorus

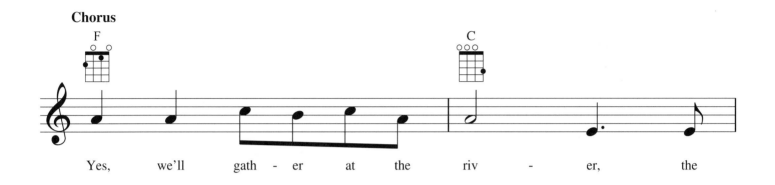

Yes,   we'll   gath - er   at   the   riv - er,   the

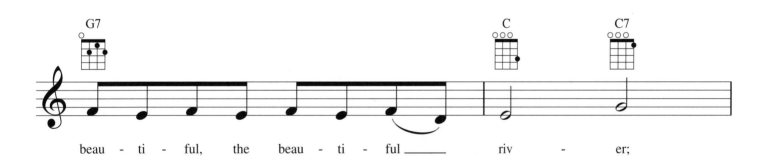

beau - ti - ful,   the   beau - ti - ful _____   riv - er;

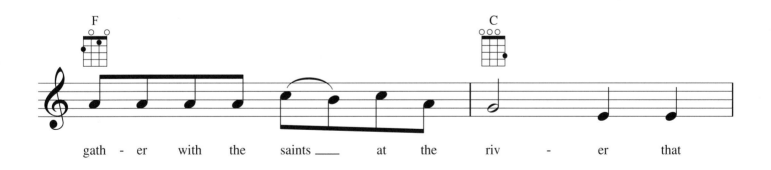

gath - er   with   the   saints _____   at   the   riv - er   that

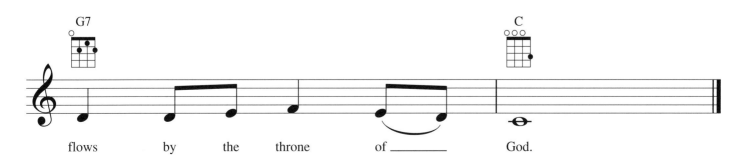

flows   by   the   throne   of _____   God.

Since Jesus Came Into My Heart

Words by Rufus H. McDaniel
Music by Charles H. Gabriel

First note

Verse
Joyfully

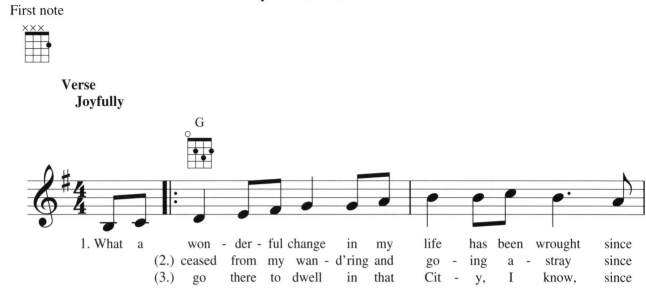

1. What a won - der - ful change in my life has been wrought since
(2.) ceased from my wan - d'ring and go - ing a - stray since
(3.) go there to dwell in that Cit - y, I know, since

Je - sus came in - to my heart. I have
Je - sus came in - to my heart. And my
Je - sus came in - to my heart. And I'm

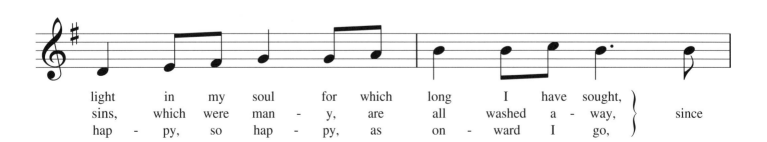

light in my soul for which long I have sought,
sins, which were man - y, are all washed a - way, } since
hap - py, so hap - py, as on - ward I go,

Je - sus came in - to my heart. Since

Chorus

Je - sus came in - to my heart, since

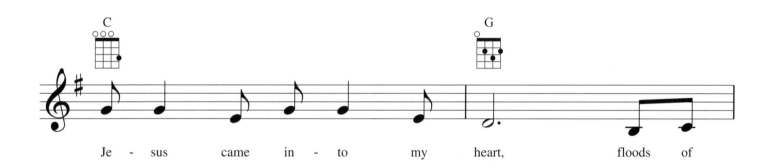

Je - sus came in - to my heart, floods of

joy o'er my soul like the sea bil - lows roll, since

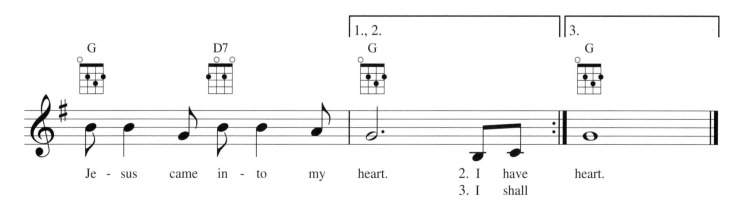

Je - sus came in - to my heart. 2. I have heart.
3. I shall

'Tis So Sweet to Trust in Jesus

Words by Louisa M.R. Stead
Music by William J. Kirkpatrick

First note

Verse
Moderately fast

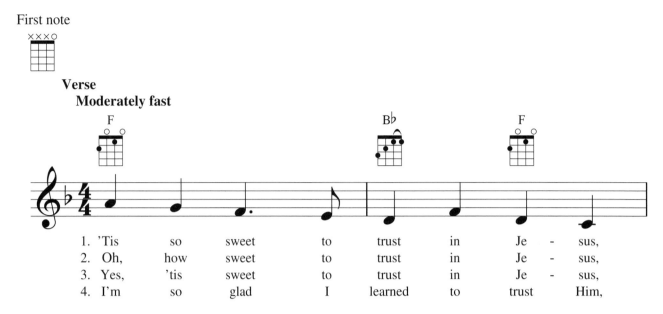

1. 'Tis   so   sweet   to   trust   in   Je - sus,
2. Oh,   how   sweet   to   trust   in   Je - sus,
3. Yes,   'tis   sweet   to   trust   in   Je - sus,
4. I'm   so   glad   I   learned to   trust Him,

just   to   take   Him   at   His   Word,
just   to   trust   His   cleans - ing   blood,
just   from   sin   and   self   to   cease,
pre - cious Je - sus,   Sav - ior,   Friend;

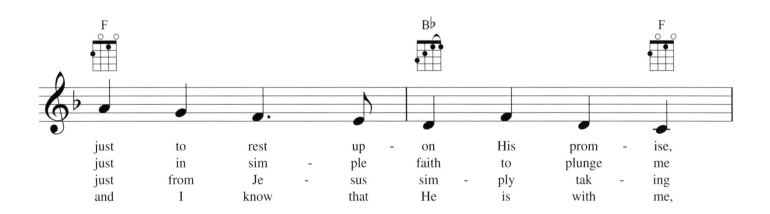

just   to   rest   up - on   His   prom - ise,
just   in   sim - ple   faith   to   plunge   me,
just   from   Je - sus   sim - ply   tak - ing,
and   I   know   that   He   is   with   me,

just to know: "Thus saith the Lord."
'neath the heal - ing, cleans - ing flood.
life and rest and joy and peace.
wilt be with me to the end.

Chorus

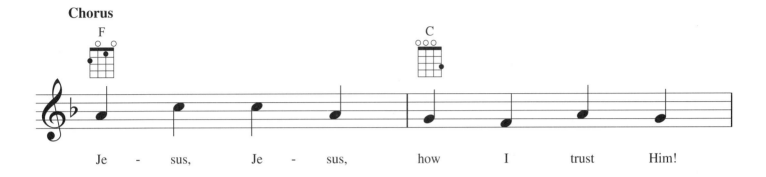

Je - sus, Je - sus, how I trust Him!

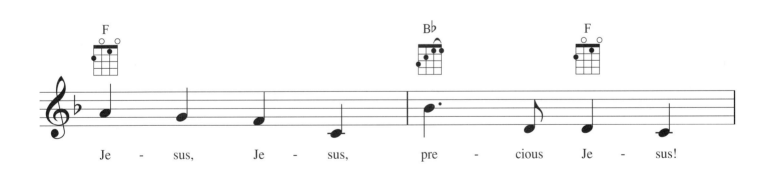

How I've proved Him o'er and o'er!

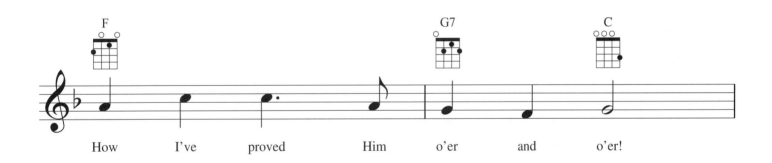

Je - sus, Je - sus, pre - cious Je - sus!

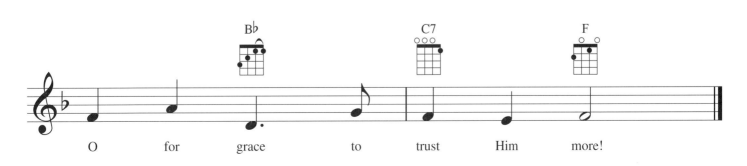

O for grace to trust Him more!

Wayfaring Stranger

Southern American Folk Hymn

First note

Verse
With longing

1. I am a poor, _____ way-far-ing stran-ger while trav-'ling
(2.) clouds _____ will gath-er 'round me, I know my
(3.) free _____ from ev-'ry tri-al, my bod-y

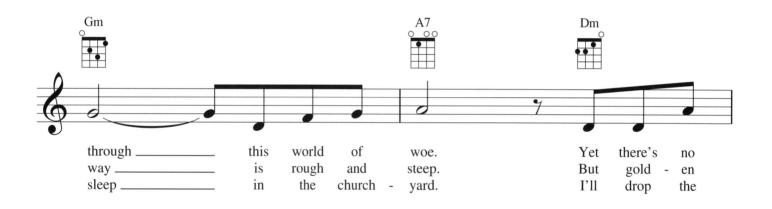

through _____ this world of woe. Yet there's no
way _____ is rough and steep. But gold-en
sleep _____ in the church-yard. I'll drop the

sick - ness, toil nor dan-ger in that bright
fields _____ lie out be-fore me where God's re -
cross _____ of self-de - ni-al and en-ter

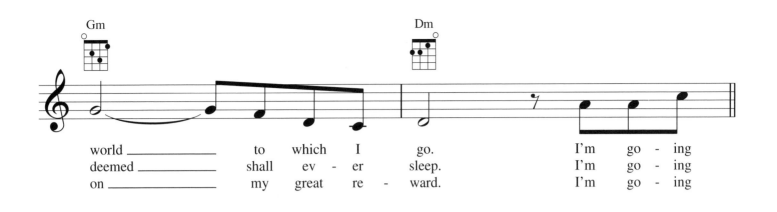

world _____ to which I go. I'm go - ing
deemed _____ shall ev - er sleep. I'm go - ing
on _____ my great re - ward. I'm go - ing

Chorus

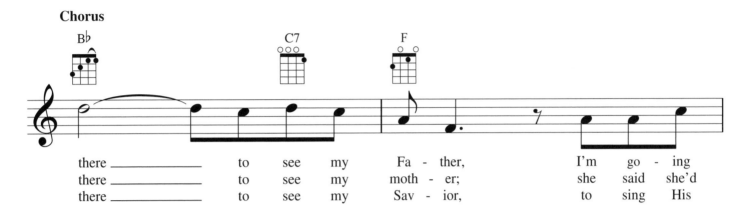

there _____ to see my Fa - ther, I'm go - ing
there _____ to see my moth - er; she said she'd
there _____ to see my Sav - ior, to sing His

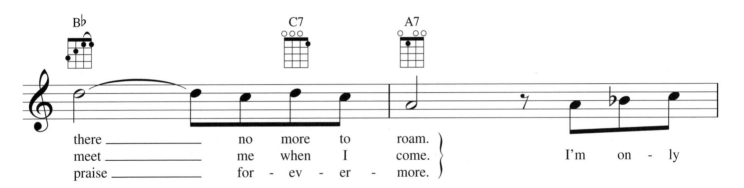

there _____ no more to roam. ⎫
meet _____ me when I come. ⎬ I'm on - ly
praise _____ for - ev - er - more. ⎭

go - ing o - ver Jor - dan, I'm on - ly

1., 2.   3.

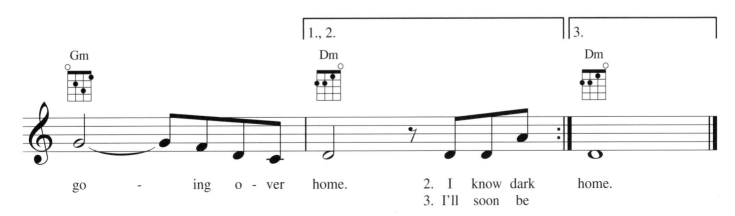

go - ing o - ver home. 2. I know dark home.
3. I'll soon be

When We All Get to Heaven

Words by Eliza E. Hewitt
Music by Emily D. Wilson

First note

1. Sing the won - drous love ____ of ____ Je - sus,
2. While we walk the pil - grim ____ path - way,
3. Let us then be true ____ and ____ faith - ful,
4. On - ward to the prize ____ be - fore us;

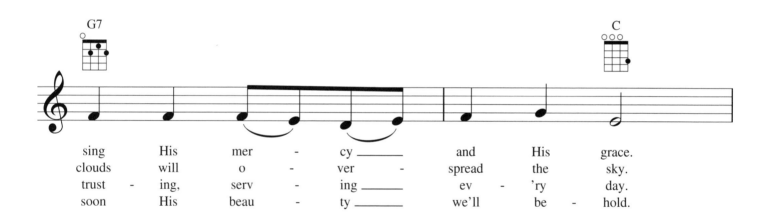

sing His mer - cy ____ and His grace.
clouds will o - ver - spread the sky.
trust - ing, serv - ing ____ ev - 'ry day.
soon His beau - ty ____ we'll be - hold.

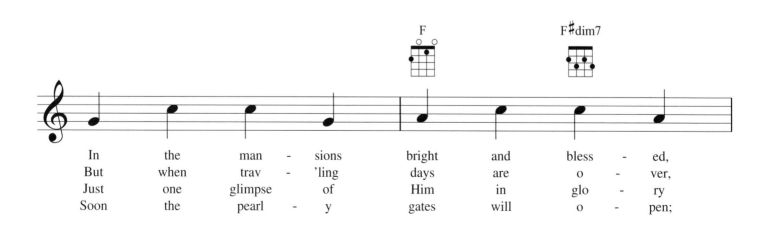

In the man - sions bright and bless - ed,
But when trav - 'ling days are o - ver,
Just one glimpse of Him in glo - ry
Soon the pearl - y gates will o - pen;

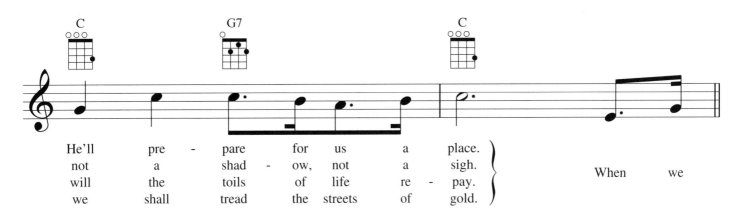

He'll   pre - pare   for   us   a   place.
not   a   shad - ow,   not   a   sigh.
will   the   toils   of   life   re - pay.
we   shall   tread   the   streets   of   gold.   When   we

Chorus

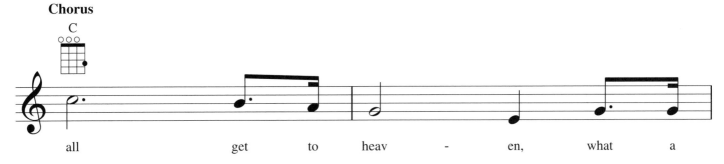

all   get   to   heav - en,   what   a

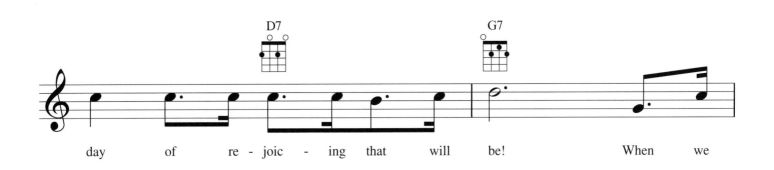

day   of   re - joic - ing   that   will   be!   When   we

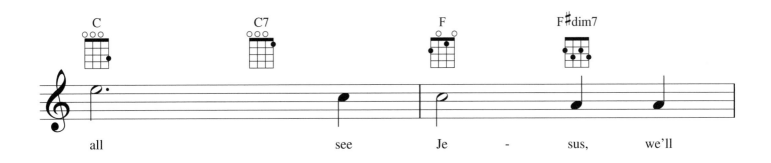

all   see   Je - sus,   we'll

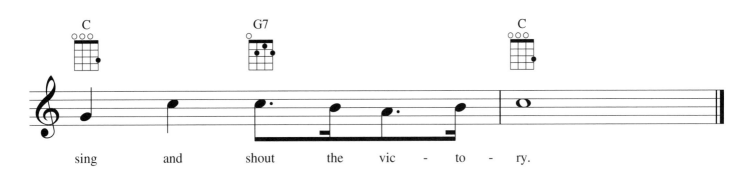

sing   and   shout   the   vic - to - ry.

Wondrous Love

Southern American Folk Hymn

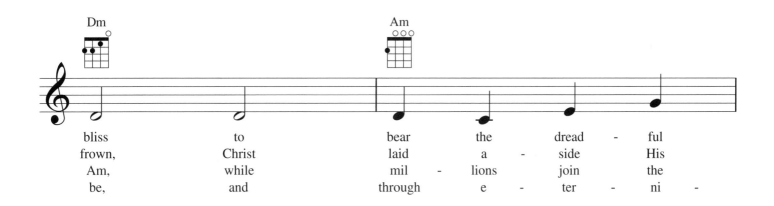

bliss	to	bear	the	dread	-	ful
frown,	Christ	laid	a	-	side	His
Am,	while	mil	-	lions	join	the
be,	and	through	e	-	ter	ni	-

curse	for	my	soul,	for	my
crown	for	my	soul,	for	my
theme,	I	will	sing,	I	will
ty	I'll	sing	on,	I'll	sing

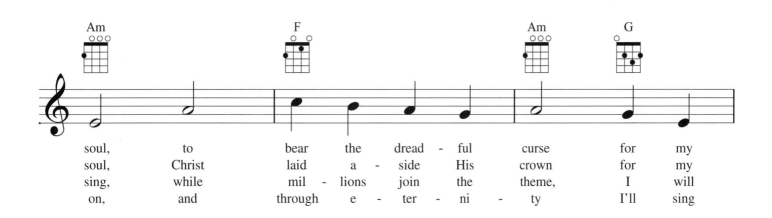

soul,	to	bear	the	dread	-	ful	curse	for	my
soul,	Christ	laid	a	-	side	His	crown	for	my
sing,	while	mil	-	lions	join	the	theme,	I	will
on,	and	through	e	-	ter	ni	-	ty	I'll	sing

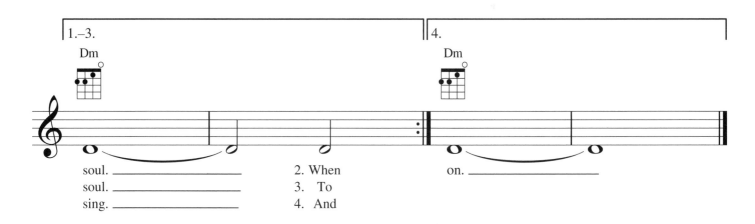

| 1.–3. | | 4. |

soul. _____	2. When	on. _____
soul. _____	3. To	
sing. _____	4. And	

The Best Collections for Ukulele

The Best Songs Ever

70 songs have now been arranged for ukulele. Includes: Always • Bohemian Rhapsody • Memory • My Favorite Things • Over the Rainbow • Piano Man • What a Wonderful World • Yesterday • You Raise Me Up • and more.

00282413........$17.99

Campfire Songs for Ukulele

30 favorites to sing as you roast marshmallows and strum your uke around the campfire. Includes: God Bless the U.S.A. • Hallelujah • The House of the Rising Sun • I Walk the Line • Puff the Magic Dragon • Wagon Wheel • You Are My Sunshine • and more.

00129170 ......$14.99

The Daily Ukulele

arr. Liz and Jim Beloff
Strum a different song everyday with easy arrangements of 365 of your favorite songs in one big songbook! Includes favorites by the Beatles, Beach Boys, and Bob Dylan, folk songs, pop songs, kids' songs, Christmas carols, and Broadway and Hollywood tunes, all with a spiral binding for ease of use.

00240356 Original Edition................$39.99
00240681 Leap Year Edition $39.99
00119270 Portable Edition $37.50

Disney Hits for Ukulele

Play 23 of your favorite Disney songs on your ukulele. Includes: The Bare Necessities • Cruella De Vil • Do You Want to Build a Snowman? • Kiss the Girl • Lava • Let It Go • Once upon a Dream • A Whole New World • and more.

00151250 ......$16.99

Also available:

00291547 **Disney Fun Songs for Ukulele** ...$16.99
00701708 **Disney Songs for Ukulele**.......$14.99
00334696 **First 50 Disney Songs on Ukulele** .$16.99

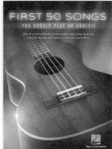

First 50 Songs You Should Play on Ukulele

An amazing collec-tion of 50 accessible, must-know favorites: Edelweiss • Hey, Soul Sister • I Walk the Line • I'm Yours • Imagine • Over the Rainbow • Peaceful Easy Feeling • The Rainbow Connection • Riptide • more.

00149250 ....$16.99

Also available:

00292082 **First 50 Melodies on Ukulele** ...$15.99
00289029 **First 50 Songs on Solo Ukulele**..$15.99
00347437 **First 50 Songs to Strum on Uke** .$16.99

40 Most Streamed Songs for Ukulele

40 top hits that sound great on uke! Includes: Despacito • Feel It Still • Girls like You • Happier • Havana • High Hopes • The Middle • Perfect • 7 Rings • Shallow • Shape of You • Something Just like This • Stay • Sucker • Sunflower • Sweet but Psycho • Thank U, Next • There's Nothing Holdin' Me Back • Without Me • and more!

00298113 ....$17.99

The 4 Chord Songbook

With just 4 chords, you can play 50 hot songs on your ukulele! Songs include: Brown Eyed Girl • Do Wah Diddy Diddy • Hey Ya! • Ho Hey • Jessie's Girl • Let It Be • One Love • Stand by Me • Toes • With or Without You • and many more.

00142050........$16.99

Also available:

00141143 **The 3-Chord Songbook**........$16.99

Pop Songs for Kids

30 easy pop favorites for kids to play on uke, including: Brave • Can't Stop the Feeling! • Feel It Still • Fight Song • Happy • Havana • House of Gold • How Far I'll Go • Let It Go • Remember Me (Ernesto de la Cruz) • Rewrite the Stars • Roar • Shake It Off • Story of My Life • What Makes You Beautiful • and more.

00284415 ....$16.99

Simple Songs for Ukulele

50 favorites for standard G-C-E-A ukulele tuning, including: All Along the Watchtower • Can't Help Falling in Love • Don't Worry, Be Happy • Ho Hey • I'm Yours • King of the Road • Sweet Home Alabama • You Are My Sunshine • and more.

00156815........$14.99

Also available:

00276644 **More Simple Songs for Ukulele** .$14.99

Top Hits of 2020

18 uke-friendly tunes of 2020 are featured in this collection of melody, lyric and chord arrangements in standard G-C-E-A tuning. Includes: Adore You (Harry Styles) • Before You Go (Lewis Capaldi) • Cardigan (Taylor Swift) • Daisies (Katy Perry) • I Dare You (Kelly Clarkson) • Level of Concern (twenty one pilots) • No Time to Die (Billie Eilish) • Rain on Me (Lady Gaga feat. Ariana Grande) • Say So (Doja Cat) • and more.

00355553 ....$14.99

Also available:

00302274 **Top Hits of 2019** $14.99

Ukulele: The Most Requested Songs

Strum & Sing Series
Cherry Lane Music
Nearly 50 favorites all expertly arranged for ukulele! Includes: Bubbly • Build Me Up, Buttercup • Cecilia • Georgia on My Mind • Kokomo • L-O-V-E • Your Body Is a Wonderland • and more.

02501453 ....$14.99

The Ultimate Ukulele Fake Book

Uke enthusiasts will love this giant, spiral-bound collection of over 400 songs for uke! Includes: Crazy • Dancing Queen • Downtown • Fields of Gold • Happy • Hey Jude • 7 Years • Summertime • Thinking Out Loud • Thriller • Wagon Wheel • and more.

00175500 9" x 12" Edition $45.00
00319997 5.5" x 8.5" Edition $39.99